THE UNITED STATES PRESIDENTS

# RONALD REAGAN

## OUR 40TH PRESIDENT

by Cynthia Amoroso

**The Child's World®**
**childsworld.com**

1980 Lookout Drive • Mankato, MN 56003-1705
800-599-READ • www.childsworld.com

## ACKNOWLEDGMENTS
**Content Adviser:** David R. Smith, Adjunct Assistant
Professor of History, University of Michigan–Ann Arbor

## PHOTOS
**Cover and page 3:** Courtesy Ronald Reagan Library (detail)
**Interior:** Associated Press, 10, 13, 14, 18, 20, 33, 38 (top right);
Bettmann via Getty Images, 29, 39 (top); Courtesy Ronald Reagan
Library, 4, 6, 7, 8, 11, 12, 16, 23, 24, 27, 32, 34, 38 (left and
bottom right), 39 (bottom); Everett Collection/Newscom, 17, 28;
Mario E. Ruiz/ZUMAPRESS/Newscom, 26; NASA, 31; PAJIC/SIPA/
Newscom, 36; Reagan.Reagan Family/ZUMAPRESS/Newscom,
5; UNIVERSAL PICTURES/Album/Newscom, 15; Walter Leporati/
Archive Photos via Getty Images, 22; © William Coupon; National
Portrait Gallery, Smithsonian Institution; gift of *Time* Magazine, 37

ISBN 9781503844315 (REINFORCED LIBRARY BINDING)
ISBN 9781503847149 (PORTABLE DOCUMENT FORMAT)
ISBN 9781503848337 (ONLINE MULTI-USER EBOOK)
LCCN 2019957740

Printed in the United States of America

# CONTENTS

*Ronald Reagan
served as president
from 1981 to 1989.*

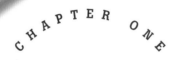

# CHAPTER ONE

# THE ROAD TO HOLLYWOOD

Ronald Reagan became president at a time when many people in the United States were worried. They were worried about going to war with other countries. They were worried about finding jobs and paying their bills. As president, Reagan worked hard to make the country stronger. Even many people who didn't agree with Reagan's policies admired him. They liked his charm, sense of humor, and friendly personality. He was a good speaker, and he always seemed to know the right thing to say, even in sad or frightening situations. Because of this, he was sometimes called the Great Communicator.

Ronald Wilson Reagan was born in Tampico, Illinois, on February 6, 1911. He was the younger of Jack and Nelle Reagan's two sons. His older brother's name was Neil. Ronald's family was poor, but his mother always took care of the family's needs. They moved a great deal when Ronald was a young child.

Ronald was a happy boy who enjoyed climbing rocks, hiking through the woods, exploring the countryside, and sledding and ice-skating in winter.

*Ronald Reagan in 1984*

*The Reagan family in 1914 or 1915: Ronald (in front of his mother), Neil, and parents Jack and Nelle. Jack Reagan had a difficult time keeping a job as a shoe salesman, and the family did not have much money.*

Most of all, he loved playing football with his friends. In school, Ronald was a successful student. Not only did learning come easily to him, but the other students liked his friendly, positive personality. By high school, the Reagan family was living in Dixon, Illinois. Ronald joined the football team when he entered North Dixon High School. Unfortunately, he was small for his age, and he sat on the bench most of the season. The following summer, he found a job working for a local construction company. The physical work helped him develop strong muscles. Ronald also started taking swimming lessons and became an excellent swimmer. Over the next few years, as he continued to swim and stay physically active, he grew stronger. He also grew tall.

**In the days after Ronald Reagan was born, his father often referred to him as his "fat little Dutchman." Soon, family and friends were referring to Ronald as "Dutch." This nickname stuck, and people called him Dutch for the rest of his life.**

**While working as a lifeguard, Reagan once rescued an elderly man's false teeth from the bottom of a pool. They had fallen out while the man was swimming!**

**Growing up, Ronald Reagan was small compared to other boys his age. When he was in high school, Ronald was 5 feet 3 inches (160 cm) tall and weighed 108 pounds (49 kg). After high school, he grew to be over 6 feet (183 cm) tall and weighed 185 pounds (84 kg).**

Reagan followed Margaret Cleaver, his high school sweetheart, to Eureka College, in Eureka, Illinois. He was excited to begin his career. "I wanted to get in that school so badly, that it hurt when I thought about it," Reagan once said. He paid his own way through college. He had saved money from a job working as a lifeguard back in Dixon. Reagan received a partial scholarship from Eureka. But the scholarship did not pay for all his needs. He also washed dishes at a **fraternity** house to help pay his bills. At Eureka, Reagan studied **economics** and **sociology.**

Reagan worked as a lifeguard at Lowell Park in Dixon, Illinois.

Ronald Reagan (far right) poses with his teammates on the Eureka College swim team.

Even with his job, Reagan found time to become involved in many activities at Eureka College. He played football, was the captain of the swim team, and was a member of the track team. Reagan also became interested in drama at Eureka. He started performing in plays and found that he loved being onstage. By the time he graduated, he had played the lead role in several plays. He worked on the school newspaper and yearbook. Ronald was also a leader, serving as student-council president during his senior year.

Reagan worked as an announcer for WHO radio station in Des Moines, Iowa, from 1934 to 1937.

After graduating in 1932, Reagan decided to pursue a career in acting. After all, communicating and speaking in front of others came easily to him. Radio was popular at that time, and he decided to try to get a job as a radio actor. He first looked for work in Chicago, Illinois, one of the biggest cities in the country. But people told him he needed to get experience in smaller towns before he could get a job in a city like Chicago. So he drove to Davenport, Iowa, hoping to find work as a sports announcer for WOC radio. The station manager gave him a chance. For 20 minutes, Reagan pretended to announce the play-by-play of a football game.

The station manager followed every play as Reagan excitedly described the action of an imaginary game. The manager was quickly convinced that young Reagan could do excellent work and offered him the job.

Reagan was successful at WOC. His humor and friendliness on the air made him a good radio announcer. Soon, he moved to a bigger station, called WHO, in Des Moines, Iowa. One of his jobs there was to announce the Chicago Cubs baseball games. Radio announcers needed a way to find out what was happening at the game. Some traveled with the team, but others did not. Reagan stayed at the station in Des Moines, even though the games were being played all over the country. He used a telegraph machine to receive the information about what was happening in the game. Someone at the game would type the information into a telegraph machine. The machine would send the information to Reagan, who had a machine with him at the station. He would quickly read the information to himself and then announce it as though he was in the middle of the action and excitement at the game. He was very good at this. In fact, listeners never knew that he wasn't actually at the game.

While working for WHO, Reagan had the opportunity to travel with the Chicago Cubs to spring training in California. There he met a Hollywood movie agent. The agent was impressed with Reagan's personality and good looks. In 1937, he arranged for Reagan to try out for a movie role.

**Reagan's first radio assignment was to announce a football game between the University of Iowa and the University of Minnesota.
He was paid five dollars and the cost of his bus ticket.**

**During his first year at Warner Brothers Studio, Reagan made 10 movies. He played radio announcers in several of these early films. These were easy roles for him because of his own radio-announcing experience.**

Reagan returned to Iowa a few days later and received a message from the agent. Reagan had been offered a movie **contract** with Warner Brothers Studio! It was a seven-year contract, starting at $200 per week. This was a lot of money for a young man at the time. Reagan accepted the offer, bought a **convertible,** and headed to Hollywood. He was popular in Hollywood. As always, people liked his warm, happy personality. They enjoyed being around him. Reagan also earned a **reputation** as a hardworking, responsible actor who was always on time and did a good job.

One day while eating lunch in the studio cafeteria, Reagan met an actress named Jane Wyman. They became friends and soon began dating. In 1940, they married. Their daughter, Maureen, was born in 1941.

*Ronald Reagan acted in a few movies with Jane Wyman (pictured), and they fell in love and got married in 1940. Shown here is a movie still from their 1940 film* Brother Rat and a Baby.

# REAGAN THE MOVIE STAR

Many US presidents have worked as lawyers or in business before entering politics. Reagan followed a different path: he was an actor. Reagan acted in more than 50 films between 1937 and 1964. He played the lead in 30 of those movies. His first film was *Love Is on the Air*, and his last film was *The Killers*. *King's Row*, which Reagan made in 1942, is considered his best film. The film was in the running for the Academy Award for Best Picture.

Reagan performed in many different kinds of movies during his career, but he is often remembered for his roles in Westerns or action and adventure movies. He also played athletes in several movies. One of Reagan's best-known roles was playing real-life Notre Dame college football player George "the Gipper" Gipp in the movie *Knute Rockne: All American* (1940). As president, Reagan sometimes behaved like the Gipper or repeated lines from the movie. His

connection with the character of George Gipp was so strong that in January 1989, officials from the University of Notre Dame presented him with a sweater that the real George Gipp had worn during his years there. The picture below shows Reagan in his role as Gipp.

# CHAPTER TWO

# A NEW CAREER

In December 1941, the United States became involved in World War II. Ronald Reagan wanted to do his part. His eyesight was not good enough to serve in combat, so he was assigned to make training films for the soldiers. In 1945, when the war ended, he returned home to Hollywood.

Ronald Reagan (seated, at left) joined the US Army Air Force in 1942. Because of his poor eyesight, he could not become a pilot. Instead, he used his acting skills and made more than 400 training films for the army.

Reagan's first wife, Jane Wyman, was a successful actress. In 1948, she won an Oscar for her role in Johnny Belinda. Ronald and Jane are shown here with their daughter, Maureen, at their Los Angeles home in 1942 as Ronald leaves to report for army duty.

That year, he and Jane adopted a son named Michael. Reagan tried to return to his movie career, but he found it difficult. Before entering the army, he had been offered roles in large films. He was a popular actor. But after returning to Hollywood, he had a hard time finding movie roles.

In 1947, Reagan became president of the Screen Actors Guild. This organization tried to improve working conditions for film actors. Reagan served as president of the Screen Actors Guild for six years. He worked to get good medical insurance and other benefits for actors. During this time, he had his first chance to speak before Congress, asking them to pass laws to help the Screen Actors Guild. This experience sparked Reagan's interest in politics.

As president of the Screen Actors Guild, Reagan was also concerned about the influence of **communism** in Hollywood. Under communism, the government controls the economy and owns most of the businesses. In the years after World War II, the United States and the **Soviet Union,** a large communist country, competed for influence around the world. Many Americans were swept up by a fear of communism. During this period, Reagan gave Congress information about actors whom he suspected supported communist governments. Reagan's concern about communism would last the rest of his life.

*Reagan spoke to members of Congress about communism in Hollywood. He told Congress that communists were a serious threat in the movie industry.*

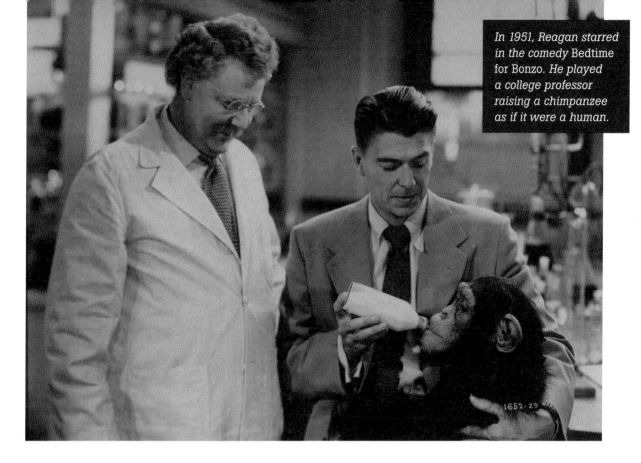

In 1951, Reagan starred in the comedy Bedtime for Bonzo. He played a college professor raising a chimpanzee as if it were a human.

In 1949 and 1950, Reagan also served as chairman of the Motion Picture Industry Council. This was an organization that worked to promote a positive image of actors and of the film business. As Reagan became more involved in the political world, he acted less and less. His political activities were taking a great deal of his time. Meanwhile, his wife was enjoying more and more success as an actress. Their interests and beliefs were moving apart. In 1949, Ronald and Jane divorced.

In the years after, Reagan took several movie parts and continued to stay active with the Screen Actors Guild. In 1951, he acted in *Bedtime for Bonzo*, a movie many people remember for the chimpanzee that was his "co-star."

*Ronald and Nancy Reagan had two children, Patricia and Ronald.*

In 1952, Reagan married an actress named Nancy Davis, and they soon had a daughter named Patricia. A son, Ronald, would follow in 1958. Although Reagan's personal life was happy during this time, his acting career had stalled.

In the 1950s, television was becoming popular. Reagan thought this might be a new opportunity for him. In 1954, he accepted an offer to host a television program called *General Electric Theater*. This show became an instant success. One of his duties as host was to visit General Electric workplaces and talk to the employees. He told the General Electric workers about being an actor and working in Hollywood.

**Nancy Davis and Ronald Reagan met in 1949. She had seen his movies and thought he was handsome and charming. After Ronald's divorce, friends introduced him to Nancy.**

He also took an interest in the company's political views and was good at talking about these views with other people.

Reagan hosted *General Electric Theater* for eight years, until the show went off the air. Then, he was hired to host *Death Valley Days*, which he did until 1965.

**Ronald Reagan injured his leg in a baseball game shortly before his first date with Nancy Davis. He arrived at her front door using crutches.**

*Reagan loved horses. His interest began in 1946, while making a movie called* Stallion Road. *Afterward, Reagan bought a ranch in Santa Barbara, California, and made a hobby of working with horses.*

By that time, Reagan's life and interests had changed. During the years he spent speaking to the workers at General Electric, Reagan had developed firm beliefs about politics and the future of the United States. He now had strong opinions about how the government should be run. Many people suggested that he run for public office. Although he didn't run in an election right away, he did help other **candidates.** Vice President Richard Nixon was running for president in the 1960 election. Nixon was a member of the Republican Party, one of the nation's two most powerful **political parties.** Reagan gave about 200 speeches in support of Nixon. But Nixon lost the election to John F. Kennedy, who was a member of the Democratic Party, the nation's other major political party.

In 1964, Senator Barry Goldwater of Arizona decided to run for president. By then, Reagan had become a leader in California's Republican Party. Reagan was one of two people in charge of Goldwater's **campaign.** To help Goldwater raise money, Reagan taped a 30-minute speech. It was called "A Time for Choosing." The speech was shown on television, and many people who saw it were impressed with Reagan. His reputation as the "Great Communicator" had begun. Other Republicans suggested that Reagan run for governor of California in 1966, and Reagan agreed.

Ronald Reagan, the Republican candidate for governor of California, shakes hands with supporters at a campaign rally in Los Angeles. He was elected governor twice, in 1966 and in 1970.

Ronald Reagan traveled all over California during his campaign. He also appeared on television. On November 8, 1966, he was elected governor of California. He felt it was important to communicate directly with the people of the state, and he often gave televised speeches. In 1970, Californians reelected Reagan as their governor.

As governor, Reagan had to deal with California's financial problems. He changed how the state government spent money. He did not hire any more state workers. He changed how the state helped people who were on **welfare.** He raised taxes to help the state government pay for what was needed. Reagan succeeded in improving the financial condition of California.

Many of Reagan's friends and supporters urged him to run for president. In 1976, he decided the time was right. But another Republican named Gerald Ford was also running. Ford was the current president, and he wanted to stay in office for another four years. Ford narrowly defeated Reagan to become the Republican Party's candidate for president. In the election, Democrat Jimmy Carter defeated Ford.

Reagan thought his chance to run for president of the United States was gone. He had no idea what his future would hold. But in fact, his career as a politician had only just begun.

**Reagan joined the Republican Party in 1962. Earlier in his life, he had been a Democrat. Growing up, Reagan had greatly admired Democratic president Franklin D. Roosevelt.**

# NANCY REAGAN

First Lady Nancy Reagan will long be remembered for being one of her husband's biggest supporters. She took great pride in Reagan's accomplishments and in being his wife. She once said, "My life really began when I married my husband."

Nancy was born in New York City on July 6, 1921. Her name at birth was Anne Frances Robbins, but her family always called her Nancy. Her family moved to Chicago when she was six. She had a happy childhood in Chicago with her mother, Edith, who was an actress, and her stepfather, Loyal Davis, who was a surgeon.

Nancy majored in theater at Smith College in Massachusetts. In college, she acted in plays and even had the chance to act on Broadway in the play *Lute Song*. She used the name Nancy Davis as her stage name. Soon, she began acting in Hollywood movies.

Nancy completed 11 movies between 1949 and 1956. Her last movie, *Hellcats of the Navy*, also starred Ronald Reagan.

After marrying Reagan, Nancy retired from show business to raise her family. When Reagan was governor of California, she became active in helping people with physical and emotional handicaps. She also lent her support to a special program for the elderly called the Foster Grandparent Program. She even wrote a book about it. In the photo below, Nancy answers questions about the Foster Grandparent program during a radio interview in 1982.

After her husband was elected president, Nancy used her position as First Lady to support the arts and to lead the fight against drug use among young people. She continued this effort long after she and her husband left the White House in 1989.

# CHAPTER THREE

# THE ROAD TO THE PRESIDENCY

Ronald Reagan was disappointed that he did not win the Republican presidential **nomination** in 1976. Some people thought that he had missed his chance to run for president. But Reagan was not discouraged. He decided to run for president again in 1980.

Reagan organized a committee in 1978 to help him with his 1980 presidential campaign. Everything seemed to be moving in the right direction. Several other candidates were also competing for the Republican nomination, including a former congressman from Texas named George H. W. Bush. After a hard-fought campaign, the Republicans nominated Reagan to be their presidential candidate. Reagan chose Bush to run for vice president.

The opponents of Reagan and Bush were President Jimmy Carter and Vice President Walter Mondale. During Carter's four years in office, the country went through economic struggles. The cost of goods had increased greatly, and more than eight million people did not have jobs.

*Some of the freed American hostages wave to the crowds of people welcoming them home during a parade in New York City on January 30, 1981. The Americans were held in Iran for 444 days.*

The United States was also experiencing some serious problems with other countries. Iranian **terrorists** were holding 52 American citizens as **hostages,** and Carter had thus far been unable to help them. During the campaign, Reagan criticized Carter for not solving these problems. Although the election was too close to call at one point, Reagan easily defeated Carter to become the nation's 40th president.

Reagan's **inauguration** took place on January 20, 1981. At the inauguration, Reagan announced that the American hostages held in Iran were being released and would soon return to freedom. Although many people credited Reagan for this, President Jimmy Carter had struggled for months to **negotiate** their release. Carter finally reached an agreement with the Iranians on January 19, 1981, the day before Reagan took office.

Shortly into Reagan's presidency, tragedy struck. On March 30, 1981, a man named John Hinckley Jr. tried to **assassinate** Reagan as he was leaving a hotel in Washington, DC. Hinckley fired six shots, wounding a police officer, a Secret Service agent, and Reagan's press secretary, James Brady. When they heard the shots, Secret Service agents pushed Reagan into his limousine. The car sped away from the scene. Only then did the agents discover that Reagan had also been wounded.

**John Hinckley Jr. had a history of mental illness, yet he was able to buy a gun. Hinckley seriously wounded press secretary James Brady during the assassination attempt. After his recovery, Brady and his wife worked to pass laws that would require waiting periods and background checks for all people who wanted to buy handguns. This law, called the Brady Bill, was finally approved in 1993.**

*President Reagan was up and smiling just four days after he was shot.*

The car rushed the president to the hospital. Doctors performed surgery to repair damage to Reagan's chest and one of his lungs. Even on the day of the shooting, Reagan kept his sense of humor. As he was brought into the operating room, he said to the surgeons, "I hope you're all Republicans." Reagan recovered quickly and returned to work less than two weeks after he was shot.

One of Reagan's greatest concerns as president was the nation's economy. His plan for improving the economy was to reduce government spending. He believed that the US government wasted a great deal of money. He also wanted to provide large tax cuts for people and businesses. News reporters referred to his economic plans as Reaganomics.

In 1983, a truck bomb killed 241 US Marines. Ronald and Nancy Reagan attended a special memorial service honoring the victims.

Many people criticized his ideas because they reduced or ended programs that helped needy people around the nation. Other people believed Reaganomics would lead the nation to a new level of success.

**In 1981, Reagan appointed Sandra Day O'Connor to the US Supreme Court. She was the first woman ever to be appointed.**

The other area of focus for Reagan during his first **term** was foreign relations, or the nation's relationships with other countries. His most important goal was to keep communism from spreading to new countries. At that time, relations were tense between the United States and the Soviet Union. The Soviets were powerful and hoped to spread their communist system to other parts of the world. Reagan spoke against the Soviet Union, calling it an "evil empire." He planned to build up the US military and increase the production of **nuclear weapons** as a show of US strength.

The United States also had tense relations with other countries. In August 1983, Reagan sent 800 US soldiers to the Middle Eastern country of Lebanon. The soldiers were part of an international peacekeeping effort in Lebanon's capital city of Beirut. People who believed in different religions—Christians and Muslims—had been at war there. Many Muslims did not like having American soldiers in Beirut. On October 23, 1983, someone drove a truck through the gates of the US Marine camp. The truck, which was filled with explosives, crashed into the main building. The truck bomb almost completely destroyed the building, killing 241 US Marines.

**Ronald and Nancy Reagan liked to watch movies in the White House theater. Sometimes, when they were not entertaining guests for dinner, they ate their meals on TV trays in front of the television.**

Two days after the explosion in Beirut, the world's attention turned to the Caribbean island of Grenada. Cuba, a communist nation and Soviet **ally,** was trying to help establish a communist government in Grenada. Reagan feared for the safety of American students in Grenada and worried about the spread of communism. He sent 1,900 US soldiers to attack Grenada. The soldiers fought Cuban and Grenadian soldiers. The battle was over in a few days. Although many people in Grenada appreciated Reagan's efforts to return peace to their country, his critics wondered whether the attack was necessary. Reagan himself was consistently committed to fighting the spread of communism and to demonstrating the strength of the United States.

US Marines land in St. George's, the capital of the island nation, during the US invasion of Grenada. About 100 people were killed during the brief war.

# REAGANOMICS

One of Ronald Reagan's main goals as president was to strengthen the economy. To do this, he came up with a plan that was nicknamed Reaganomics.

The heart of Reagan's plan was to have the government spend less money. Many people believe the government should provide programs to help those in need. These programs cost a lot of money. The money the government spends comes from the taxes people pay.

Reagan didn't think that these programs were helping people the way they should. He didn't want the government to continue providing such expensive programs if they weren't working well. If the programs were cut back, people would not have to pay so much in taxes. Reagan believed that if people got to keep more of their money, they would spend more money. When people spend money, businesses grow, and more jobs are created. With more jobs and a stronger economy, people would no longer need government programs to help them.

After Reagan put his plan into effect, businesses and wealthier people paid less in taxes. Many people credit Reagan with a boom in business. But Reagan's plan also pushed the nation into deep debt. Because he cut taxes, the government had less money. But he also oversaw a huge increase in military spending. As a result, the government spent far more money than it had. Reagan's plan may not have been as successful as he had hoped, but he left his mark on America's economy. He will always be remembered for Reaganomics.

# "FOUR MORE YEARS"

In 1984, it was time for Reagan to consider whether to run for another term as president. His popularity was high, and his supporters sometimes chanted "Four More Years" to encourage him to run for president once again.

Reagan decided to run for reelection. George H. W. Bush would again run for vice president. The Democratic candidate for president was Walter Mondale, who had been vice president under Jimmy Carter. The Democrat's vice presidential candidate was Geraldine Ferraro, a member of the House of Representatives. She was the first woman ever nominated to run for vice president of the United States by a major political party. Reagan easily defeated Mondale in the election. He would serve as the nation's president for another four years.

As Reagan began his second term, he faced difficulties with the North African country of Libya and its leader, Muammar al-Qaddafi. Tensions between the two countries had been high for some time.

*Ronald Reagan campaigned for reelection in 1984.*

Crowds cheer President Reagan and Vice President Bush at the 1984 Republican National Convention. *In the election, Reagan won 49 of the 50 states.*

In 1981, US military planes had shot down two Libyan fighter jets over the Gulf of Sidra. Libya claimed the gulf as its territory; the United States disputed this. As the 1980s progressed, Libya openly supported terrorist groups that targeted Americans. Some Libyans were involved in bombings and **hijackings.**

While dealing with Libya and other important issues, Reagan faced a personal crisis. In July 1985, doctors discovered he had cancer. They performed surgery to remove a tumor. The surgery was a success, and he recovered quickly and returned to work.

**In 1980, at 69 years old, Reagan became the oldest person ever elected president. Donald Trump broke that record in 2016. Trump was 70 years old when he was elected the 45th president of the United States.**

**Reagan loved jellybeans. As governor and as president, he always had a jar of jellybeans on his desk.**

**Reagan often answered reporters' questions with the presidential helicopter roaring in the background (as it readied to take off). This was an attempt to keep the question-and-answer sessions short.**

As 1985 ended, the situation between the United States and Libya remained tense. Reagan called Libya's support of terrorist groups "armed **aggression** against the United States." In April 1986, Reagan decided to use military force. In a surprise attack, US military planes dropped bombs on two Libyan cities. Relations with Libya would continue to haunt Reagan throughout his second term.

Another significant incident during Reagan's second term was the *Challenger* disaster. In January 1986, NASA prepared to send the space shuttle *Challenger* into space. This mission was unusual because Christa McAuliffe, a teacher, was part of the crew. She was the first person to be sent into space who was not a trained astronaut. Shortly after takeoff, *Challenger* exploded, killing everyone onboard. The incident shocked the nation. In honoring the *Challenger* crew, Reagan delivered one of his most memorable speeches. "We will never forget them," said Reagan, "nor the last time we saw them—this morning, as they prepared for their journey, and waved good-bye, and slipped the surly bonds of earth to touch the face of God."

US schoolteacher Christa McAuliffe (front center) undergoes zero gravity training while preparing for her historic spaceflight. Teacher Barbara Morgan (second from right) was McAuliffe's backup in the Teacher in Space program. Morgan would eventually complete the mission in 2007 on the shuttle Endeavour, becoming the first educator astronaut to reach orbit.

The last few words were from a poem by John Gillespie Magee Jr. about the beauty of flying. Magee was a pilot who died in World War II. Reagan's heartfelt speech helped Americans deal with the sadness they felt.

Relations with the Soviet Union were another focus of Reagan's second term. During his first term, Reagan had been outspoken in his belief that the Soviet Union needed to change its form of government and end communism. The government of the Soviet Union maintained firm control over the Soviet people and denied them basic rights, such as the right to leave the country or practice their religion. Individuals could not even own businesses. Instead, they all belonged to the government. Reagan believed that individuals should have greater freedom.

In March 1985, Mikhail Gorbachev became the Soviet Union's leader. Gorbachev wanted to improve his country's relationship with the United States, and he and Reagan met several times. On June 12, 1987, Reagan gave a speech in the German city of Berlin. A tall wall divided the city in two. On one side of the Berlin Wall was East Germany, a nation closely tied to the Soviet Union. On the other side was West Berlin, which was part of West Germany, a country closely tied to the United States. The Berlin Wall kept East Germans from escaping to West Germany and kept outsiders from entering East Germany with-

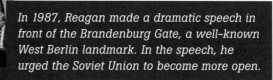

out permission. To the rest of the world, this wall represented the lack of freedom under communist rule.

During his speech on June 12, 1987, President Reagan stood near the Berlin Wall and challenged Gorbachev to change the government of the Soviet Union. "Mr. Gorbachev," Reagan demanded, "open this gate . . . tear down this wall!" The governments of the Soviet Union and East Germany were in fact losing power. Protests against them were growing.

*In 1987, Reagan made a dramatic speech in front of the Brandenburg Gate, a well-known West Berlin landmark. In the speech, he urged the Soviet Union to become more open.*

*President Reagan and Soviet leader Mikhail Gorbachev (left) sign the Intermediate-Range Nuclear Forces Treaty during a ceremony in the White House East Room in 1987. The United States and Soviet Union agreed to eliminate their supplies of certain types of missiles that could carry nuclear weapons.*

Later that year, Gorbachev visited the United States. Previous meetings between Reagan and Gorbachev had focused on the weapons that each country had. The United States was worried because the Soviet Union had nuclear weapons. The Soviet Union was worried because the United States had them, too. So far, the two leaders had been unable to make a deal on controlling the number of weapons each country had.

The American people were glad that Gorbachev was visiting the United States. They hoped it was a sign that peace was possible between the United States and the Soviet Union. Gorbachev was friendly to the American people. They welcomed him. While he and Reagan disagreed about weapons, they respected one another and had begun developing a friendship. That friendship helped the two leaders reach an agreement. In Washington, DC, on December 8, 1987, they signed an agreement called the Intermediate-Range Nuclear Forces **Treaty.** The treaty eliminated one major type of nuclear weapon. This was a big step in improving relations between the two nations.

Two years later, the communist governments in the Soviet Union and East Germany collapsed, and the Berlin Wall was torn down. A piece of the wall was presented to Reagan on April 12, 1990. It is now on display at the Ronald W. Reagan Presidential Library and Museum in Simi Valley, California.

Over the years, Reagan and Gorbachev became personal friends. In the spring of 1992, Gorbachev visited California, and Reagan referred to him as a friend and a "great man." At the Reagan Presidential Library and Museum, Reagan presented Gorbachev with the first Ronald Reagan Freedom Award.

One of the most difficult events of Reagan's second term was the Iran-Contra affair. Some of Reagan's advisers had sold weapons to Iran and were using the money to fight the government in the Central American nation of Nicaragua. The people fighting against the government of Nicaragua were called the Contras. Laws barred the US government from both selling weapons to Iran and from directly funding the Contras.

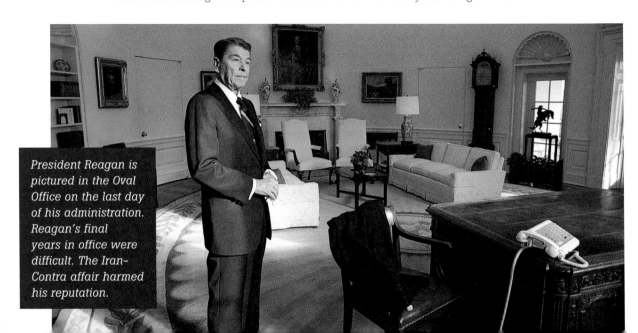

President Reagan is pictured in the Oval Office on the last day of his administration. Reagan's final years in office were difficult. The Iran-Contra affair harmed his reputation.

When it came out that the Reagan administration had done both, investigations began. Several members of Reagan's staff were forced to leave their jobs. Many people wondered how much President Reagan and Vice President Bush knew about the Iran-Contra affair. For a time, his popularity plummeted, but he regained support by the end of his term.

US presidents can serve only two terms, so Reagan did not run for reelection in 1988. He left office in January 1989, at the age of 77. He had often called the United States a "shining city on a hill" and did so again in his final presidential speech. "My friends," said Reagan, "We did it. We weren't just marking time. We made a difference. We made the city stronger, we made the city freer, and we left her in good hands. All in all, not bad, not bad at all." Afterward, Ronald and Nancy Reagan returned to California to live.

In the early 1990s, Reagan was diagnosed with **Alzheimer's disease,** a devastating illness that affects a person's brain and memory. After that time, Reagan made few public appearances, spending most of his time with his family in California.

**Nancy Reagan sponsored a drive against drugs and alcohol called "Just Say No." The effort was aimed at young people.**

**Reagan loved baseball. Three times during his presidency, he threw out the first pitch at a baseball game to start the new season.**

Members of the military escort Reagan's casket in 2004. Thousands of people lined the streets of Washington, DC, to pay their last respects to the late president.

On June 5, 2004, Reagan died at age 93. The nation spent the next six days in mourning. Tens of thousands of people visited Reagan's casket, first in California, and then in the Capitol in Washington, DC. On Friday, June 11, Reagan received a state funeral, a special ceremony held only for presidents and a few others. It is one of the highest honors the United States can give.

More than 700 people attended Reagan's funeral, which was held at the Washington National Cathedral. After the funeral, Reagan's family flew with his casket back to California. He was buried during a sunset service in Simi Valley, on the grounds of the Ronald W. Reagan Presidential Library and Museum.

Reagan himself gave Americans words to remember him by: "Whatever else history may say about me when I'm gone, I hope it will record that I appealed to your best hopes, not your worst fears; to your confidence rather than your doubts. My dream is that you will travel the road ahead with liberty's lamp guiding your steps and opportunity's arm steadying your way."

# RONALD W. REAGAN PRESIDENTIAL LIBRARY AND MUSEUM

The Ronald W. Reagan Presidential Library and Museum is located in Simi Valley, California. Five American presidents–Reagan, Richard Nixon, Gerald Ford, Jimmy Carter, and George H. W. Bush–attended the dedication of the library on November 4, 1991.

Like other libraries, the Reagan Library has many written works, including books, speeches, and government documents. The Reagan Library also has 19 museum galleries that focus on different aspects of Reagan's life.

On September 20, 2004, a Boeing 747 was delivered to the Reagan Library. It had served seven different presidents as *Air Force One*, the president's private jet. The plane is now on display. Visitors can walk inside it and see exactly what it looked like when Reagan was president. Also on display is a group presidential limousines and vehicles, and a helicopter that was used to transport presidents.

Reagan is buried on the library grounds. His own words are inscribed at his gravesite: "I know in my heart that man is good, that what is right will always eventually triumph and there is purpose and worth to each and every life."

# TIME LINE

| 1910–1920 | 1930 | 1940 | 1950 | 1960 |
|---|---|---|---|---|

**1911**
Ronald Wilson Reagan is born to Jack and Nelle Reagan on February 6 in Tampico, Illinois. He is the younger of two boys.

**1920**
The Reagan family moves to Dixon, Illinois.

**1928**
Reagan graduates from North Dixon High School.

**1932**
Reagan graduates from Eureka College. He is hired to announce University of Iowa football games for a radio station in Davenport, Iowa.

**1934**
Reagan becomes the main sports announcer for radio station WHO in Des Moines, Iowa.

**1937**
Reagan is offered his first acting contract. He moves to Los Angeles and appears in his first movie, *Love Is on the Air*.

**1940**
Reagan appears in *Knute Rockne: All American*. He marries actress Jane Wyman.

**1941**
The United States enters World War II.

**1942**
Reagan joins the US Army Air Force.

**1945**
World War II ends. Reagan returns to Los Angeles and resumes his acting career.

**1947**
Reagan serves his first term as president of the Screen Actors Guild.

**1949**
Reagan and Jane Wyman divorce.

**1952**
Reagan marries actress Nancy Davis.

**1954**
Reagan begins hosting the television show *General Electric Theater*.

**1962**
Reagan joins the Republican Party.

**1964**
Reagan makes a televised speech in support of politician Barry Goldwater.

**1966**
Reagan runs for governor of California. He wins the election and serves until 1974.

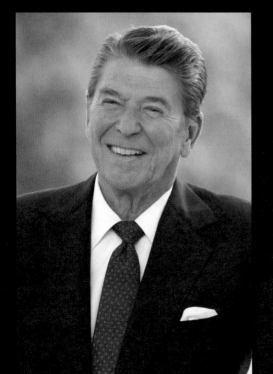

### 1976
Reagan runs for the Republican nomination for president of the United States, but the party chooses Gerald Ford instead.

### 1980
Reagan is chosen to be the Republican presidential candidate. The vice presidential candidate is George H. W. Bush. In November, Reagan and Bush win the election, defeating President Jimmy Carter and Vice President Walter Mondale.

### 1981
Reagan is inaugurated on January 20. On March 30, John Hinckley Jr. shoots Reagan in Washington, DC. Reagan is released from the hospital 12 days after the shooting. Reagan persuades Congress to pass a large tax cut.

### 1983
On October 23, 241 US Marines are killed in a bombing in Beirut, Lebanon. On October 25, Reagan orders US military troops to attack the island of Grenada.

### 1985
In January, Reagan is inaugurated for a second term as president of the United States. Mikhail Gorbachev becomes leader of the Soviet Union in March. In July, doctors discover Reagan has cancer.

### 1986
In January, the space shuttle *Challenger* explodes after liftoff, killing all seven people aboard. In April, Reagan orders US military planes to bomb Libya. The Iran-Contra scandal begins and it becomes known that top government officials illegally sold weapons to Iran and used the money to fund anti-communist rebels in Nicaragua.

### 1987
In December, Reagan and Gorbachev sign a treaty in which both nations promise to reduce the number of nuclear weapons they hold.

### 1988
Vice President George H. W. Bush is elected president.

### 1989
Reagan leaves office at the age of 77.

### 1991
The Ronald W. Reagan Presidential Library and Museum opens in Simi Valley, California.

### 1994
Reagan announces that he has Alzheimer's disease.

### 2004
Ronald Wilson Reagan dies on June 5 in Bel-Air, California, at the age of 93.

# GLOSSARY

**aggression** (uh-GREH-shun): Aggression is a threatening or violent action against someone. Libya supported terrorists who committed aggression against the United States.

**ally** (AL-lie): An ally is a nation that has agreed to help another by fighting together against a common enemy. Cuba was an ally of the Soviet Union.

**Alzheimer's disease** (ALTS-hy-murz di-ZEEZ): Alzheimer's disease is a brain disease that causes memory loss. Reagan was diagnosed with Alzheimer's disease in the early 1990s.

**assassinate** (uh-SASS-ih-nayt): Assassinate means to murder someone, especially a well-known person. John Hinckley Jr. attempted to assassinate President Reagan.

**campaign** (kam-PAYN): A campaign is the process of running for an election, including activities such as giving speeches or attending rallies. Reagan was in charge of Barry Goldwater's campaign in 1964.

**candidates** (KAN-duh-dayts): Candidates are people who are running in an election. Before he ran for office, Reagan helped other Republican candidates.

**communism** (KOM-yuh-ni-zum): Communism is a system in which the government controls the economy and owns all property. Reagan wanted to stop the spread of communism.

**contract** (KAHN-trakt): A contract is a legal agreement between two or more people. Reagan's first movie contract paid him $200 per week.

**convention** (kun-VEN-shun): A convention is a meeting. The Democratic and Republican political parties hold national conventions every four years to choose their presidential candidates.

**convertible** (kun-VUR-tuh-bul): A convertible is a car that has a top that can be lowered or removed. Reagan bought a convertible when Warner Brothers Studios gave him a movie contract.

**economics** (ek-uh-NAH-miks): Economics is the study of how people make, buy, and sell goods and services. Reagan studied economics in college.

**fraternity** (frah-TUR-nuh-tee): A fraternity is an organization of male students. Reagan helped pay for college by washing dishes at a fraternity house.

**hijackings** (HY-jak-ings): Hijackings are when someone takes control of an airplane by force. Some Libyans were involved in hijackings in the 1980s.

**hostages** (HOS-tij-ez): Hostages are people held prisoner until some demand is agreed to. Iranian terrorists held 52 American hostages from 1979 until 1981.

**inauguration** (ih-naw-gyuh-RAY-shun): An inauguration is the ceremony that takes place when a new president begins a term. Reagan's first inauguration took place on January 20, 1981.

**negotiate** (neh-GOH-shee-ayt): When people negotiate, they discuss an issue to try to come to an agreement. President Carter tried to negotiate the release of the American hostages in Iran.

**nomination** (nom-ih-NAY-shun): If someone receives a nomination, he or she is chosen by a political party to run for an office. Reagan first won the Republican presidential nomination in 1980.

**nuclear weapons** (NOO-klee-ur WEH-punz): Nuclear weapons are weapons that produce hot, powerful explosions, resulting in terrible destruction. Reagan wanted to increase the production of nuclear weapons to show that the United States could defend itself.

**political parties** (puh-LIT-uh-kul PAR-teez):Political parties are groups of people who share similar ideas about how to run a government. The Republican Party is one of the two most powerful political parties in the United States.

**politics** (PAWL-uh-tiks): Politics refers to the actions and practices of the government. Reagan first became interested in politics while working for the Screen Actors Guild.

**reputation** (reh-pyuh-TAY-shun): A reputation is how a person is seen or judged by other people. Reagan had a reputation as a hardworking actor.

**sociology** (soh-see-AH-luh-jee): Sociology is the study of society and how groups of people behave. Reagan studied sociology in college.

**Soviet Union** (SOH-vee-et YOON-yun): The Soviet Union was a communist country that stretched from eastern Europe across Asia. It broke apart into several smaller countries in 1991.

**term** (TERM): A term is the length of time a politician can keep his or her position by law. A US president's term is four years.

**terrorists** (TAYR-ur-ists): Terrorists are people who use fear and violence to force others to do something. Terrorists in Iran released 52 American hostages in 1981.

**treaty** (TREE-tee): A treaty is a formal agreement between nations. In 1987, Reagan and Gorbachev signed a treaty agreeing to do away with one kind of nuclear weapon.

**welfare** (WEL-fayr): Welfare is aid given to needy people. As governor, Reagan changed the welfare rules in California.

# THE UNITED STATES GOVERNMENT

The United States government is divided into three equal branches: the executive, the legislative, and the judicial. This division helps prevent abuses of power because each branch has to answer to the other two. No one branch can become too powerful.

## EXECUTIVE BRANCH

President
Vice President
Departments

The job of the executive branch is to enforce the laws. It is headed by the president, who serves as the spokesperson for the United States around the world. The president has the power to sign bills into law. He or she also appoints important officials, such as federal judges, who are then confirmed by the US Senate. The president is also the commander in chief of the US military. He or she is assisted by the vice president, who takes over if the president dies or cannot carry out the duties of the office.

The executive branch also includes various departments, each focused on a specific topic. They include the Defense Department, the Justice Department, and the Agriculture Department. The department heads, along with other officials such as the vice president, serve as the president's closest advisers, called the cabinet.

## LEGISLATIVE BRANCH

Congress: Senate and the
House of Representatives

The job of the legislative branch is to make the laws. It consists of Congress, which is divided into two parts: the Senate and the House of Representatives. The Senate has 100 members, and the House of Representatives has 435 members. Each state has two senators. The number of representatives a state has varies depending on the state's population.

Besides making laws, Congress also passes budgets and enacts taxes. In addition, it is responsible for declaring war, maintaining the military, and regulating trade with other countries.

## JUDICIAL BRANCH

Supreme Court
Courts of Appeals
District Courts

The job of the judicial branch is to interpret the laws. It consists of the nation's federal courts. Trials are held in district courts. During trials, judges must decide what laws mean and how they apply. Courts of appeals review the decisions made in district courts.

The nation's highest court is the Supreme Court. If someone disagrees with a court of appeals ruling, he or she can ask the Supreme Court to review it. The Supreme Court may refuse. The Supreme Court makes sure that decisions and laws do not violate the Constitution.

# CHOOSING THE PRESIDENT

It may seem odd, but American voters don't elect the president directly. Instead, the president is chosen using what is called the Electoral College.

Each state gets as many votes in the Electoral College as its combined total of senators and representatives in Congress. For example, Iowa has two senators and four representatives, so it gets six electoral votes. Although the District of Columbia does not have any voting members in Congress, it gets three electoral votes. Usually, the candidate who wins the most votes in any given state receives all of that state's electoral votes.

To become president, a candidate must get more than half of the Electoral College votes. There are a total of 538 votes in the Electoral College, so a candidate needs 270 votes to win. If nobody receives 270 Electoral College votes, the House of Representatives chooses the president.

With the Electoral College system, the person who receives the most votes nationwide does not always receive the most electoral votes. This happened most recently in 2016, when Hillary Clinton received nearly 2.9 million more national votes than Donald J. Trump. Trump became president because he had more Electoral College votes.

# THE WHITE HOUSE

The White House is the official home of the president of the United States. It is located at 1600 Pennsylvania Avenue NW in Washington, DC. In 1792, a contest was held to select the architect who would design the president's home. James Hoban won. Construction took eight years.

The first president, George Washington, never lived in the White House. The second president, John Adams, moved into the house in 1800, though the inside was not yet complete. During the War of 1812, British soldiers burned down much of the White House. It was rebuilt several years later.

The White House was changed through the years. Porches were added, and President Theodore Roosevelt added the West Wing. President William Taft changed the shape of the presidential office, making it into the famous Oval Office. While Harry Truman was president, the old house was discovered to be structurally weak. All the walls were reinforced with steel, and the rooms were rebuilt.

Today, the White House has 132 rooms (including 35 bathrooms), 28 fireplaces, and 3 elevators. It takes 570 gallons of paint to cover the outside of the six-story building. The White House provides the president with many ways to relax. It includes a putting green, a jogging track, a swimming pool, a basketball and tennis court, and beautifully landscaped gardens. The White House also has a movie theater, a billiard room, and a one-lane bowling alley.

# PRESIDENTIAL PERKS

The job of president of the United States is challenging. It is probably one of the most stressful jobs in the world. Because of this, presidents are paid well, though not nearly as well as the leaders of large corporations. In 2020, the president earned $400,000 a year. Presidents also receive extra benefits that make the demanding job a little more appealing.

★ **Camp David:** In the 1940s, President Franklin D. Roosevelt chose this heavily wooded spot in the mountains of Maryland to be the presidential retreat, where presidents can relax. Even though it is a retreat, world business is conducted there. Most famously, President Jimmy Carter met with Middle Eastern leaders at Camp David in 1978. The result was a peace agreement between Israel and Egypt.

★ *Air Force One:* The president flies on a jet called *Air Force One*. It is a Boeing 747-200B that has been modified to meet the president's needs. *Air Force One* is the size of a large home. It is equipped with a dining room, sleeping quarters, a conference room, and office space. It also has two kitchens that can provide food for up to 100 people.

★ **The Secret Service:** While not the most glamorous of the president's perks, the Secret Service is one of the most important. The Secret Service is a group of highly trained agents who protect the president and the president's family.

★ **The Presidential State Car:** The presidential state car is a customized Cadillac limousine. It has been armored to protect the president in case of attack. Inside the plush car are a foldaway desk, an entertainment center, and a communications console.

★ **The Food:** The White House has five chefs who will make any food the president wants. The White House also has an extensive wine collection and vegetable and fruit gardens.

★ **Retirement:** A former president receives a pension, or retirement pay, of just under $208,000 a year. Former presidents also receive health care coverage and Secret Service protection for the rest of their lives.

## QUALIFICATIONS

To run for president, a candidate must

★ be at least 35 years old

★ be a citizen who was born in the United States

★ have lived in the United States for 14 years

## TERM OF OFFICE

A president's term of office is four years. No president can stay in office for more than two terms.

## ELECTION DATE

The presidential election takes place every four years on the first Tuesday after November 1.

## INAUGURATION DATE

Presidents are inaugurated on January 20.

## OATH OF OFFICE

I do solemnly swear I will faithfully execute the office of the President of the United States and will to the best of my ability preserve, protect, and defend the Constitution of the United States.

## WRITE A LETTER TO THE PRESIDENT

One of the best things about being a US citizen is that Americans get to participate in their government. They can speak out if they feel government leaders aren't doing their jobs. They can also praise leaders who are going the extra mile. Do you have something you'd like the president to do? Should the president worry more about the environment and the effects of climate change? Should the government spend more money on our schools? You can write a letter to the president to say how you feel!

> 1600 Pennsylvania Avenue NW
> Washington, DC 20500

You can even write a message to the president at **whitehouse.gov/contact**.

# FOR MORE INFORMATION

## BOOKS

Medina, Nico, and Stephen Marchesi (illustrator). *What Was the Berlin Wall?* New York, NY: Penguin Workshop, 2019.

Price-Wright, Heather. *Ronald Reagan: The Great Communicator*. Huntington Beach, CA: Teacher Created Materials, 2019.

Rubinstein, Justine. *The Republican Party*. Philadelphia, PA: Mason Crest, 2020.

Shea, Therese M. *Before Ronald Reagan Was President*. New York, NY: Gareth Stevens, 2019.

Van Zee, Amy. *Nancy Reagan: Drug Crusader*. Mankato, MN: The Child's World, 2018.

## INTERNET SITES

Visit our website for lots of links about
Ronald Reagan and other US presidents:

### childsworld.com/links

*Note to Parents, Teachers, and Librarians: We routinely verify our web links to make sure they are safe, active sites. Encourage your readers to check them out!*

# INDEX